A very special Rabbit

Jakki Wood

W
FRANKLIN WATTS
LONDON • SYDNEY

If you choose me to be your rabbit –

I'm sure we'll soon be friends.

I will need my own special home called a hutch. Hutches have two rooms — one room for playing and eating,

and one room for sleeping. Fill it with clean straw so I can make a cosy nest.

I hate getting too cold or hot.
My hutch should be away from hot sun
and icy winds.

Remember to check my hutch every day
and throw out any leftover food.
Please wash it out at least once a week.

As well as my hutch I will need...

carrying box

brush and comb

hay and sawdust to go
inside my hutch

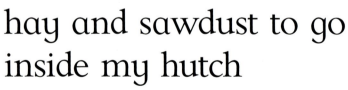

 heavy food bowl

 mineral lick

 water bottle

hay in a hay rack. Hay is an important part of a rabbit's food. I need to eat it every day.

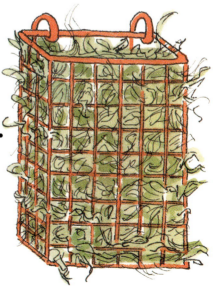

log to gnaw on. This keeps my teeth healthy and strong.

I need two meals a day. One should be special rabbit pellets. For my other meal I like fresh vegetables like cabbage, lettuce or carrots.

I love munching apples!

I also like to eat some weeds that grow outside. Don't forget I need fresh water every day.

dandelion   clover   plantain   chickweed

I love digging, but make sure I don't escape and get lost.

We can play together. My back legs are very strong, so I'm good at running,

hopping and jumping.

When you're not around I would still like to play outside. I need lots of exercise so I don't get fat. If I have a special run I can safely play out on my own.

Remember to use both hands when you pick me up. One hand to hold me around the back of my neck and the other to support me underneath.

Now scoop me up into your arms.

If I lick you it means I really like you.
I'm glad you chose me to be your friend.

A few words for parents

Taking a new pet into your home is a very important step for your family. This book will help you to tell your children how they can help settle a rabbit into its new home. This may also be a first pet for you. You are taking on responsibility for this new member of your family.

As soon as you get your rabbit, it is wise to ask your vet's advice about caring for your new pet. If you keep your rabbit outside and wild rabbits can come into your garden, your vet will advise about any necessary vaccinations. Rabbits' teeth grow continuously but normally they are kept worn down to the correct length as the rabbit gnaws its food. If the teeth are damaged they may grow too long and should be trimmed by your vet. Their claws may also grow too long and will need trimming.

Do check your rabbit every day. It is vital to keep the coat clean. This is especially important in warm weather. If the coat becomes soiled then flies may be attracted and can lay their eggs on the soiled coat. The eggs will hatch into maggots. With proper care this should not happen, but, if it does, seek urgent veterinary care.

Don't leave your rabbit continuously shut up in a hutch. If you can be with your rabbit and your garden is well-fenced, then you can let it run around for a while. Otherwise, do let the rabbit spend some time each day in a run. The bottom of the run should have mesh so that the rabbit cannot burrow out.

Do train your children always to wash their hands after playing with the rabbit and especially before they eat any food.

Enjoy your rabbit.

Terence Bate BVSc, LLB, MRCVS

Sharing books with your child

Me and My World are a range of books for you to share with your child. Together you can look at the pictures and talk about the subject or story. Listening, looking and talking are the first vital stages in children's reading development, and lay the early foundation for good reading habits.

Talking about the pictures is the first step in involving children in the pages of a book, especially if the subject or story can be related to their own familiar world. When children can relate the matter in the book to their own experience, this can be used as a starting point for introducing new knowledge, whether it is counting, getting to know colours or finding out how other people live.

Gradually children will develop their listening and concentration skills as well as a sense of what a book is. Soon they will learn how a book works: that you turn the pages from right to left, and read the story from left to right on a double page. They start to realize that the black marks on the page have a meaning and that they relate to the pictures. Once children have grasped these basic essentials they will develop strategies for "decoding" the text such as matching words and pictures, and recognising the rhythm of the language in order to predict what comes next. Soon they will start to take on the role of an independent reader, handling and looking at books even if they can't yet read the words.

Most important of all, children should realize that books are a source of pleasure. This stems from your reading sessions which are times of mutual enjoyment and shared experience. It is then that children find the key to becoming real readers.

This edition 2003

Franklin Watts
96 Leonard Street,
London EC2A 4XD

Franklin Watts Australia
45-51 Huntley Street
Alexandria NSW 2015

ISBN 0 7496 5056 7

A CIP catalogue record for this book is available from the British Library

First published as *If you choose me Rabbit* in the Early Worms series

Printed in Belgium

Consultant advice: Sue Robson and Alison Kelly,
Senior Lecturers in Education,
Faculty of Education, Early Childhood Centre,
Roehampton Institute, London.
Veterinary advice: Terence Bate BVSc, LLB, MRCVS